Deliverance from the Stronghold of Suicide

Dr. Taquetta Baker

Kingdom Wellness Counseling and Mentoring Center

Christian Counseling

SOAR INTO EMOTIONAL WELLNESS

Dr. TAQUETTA BAKER

Kingdom Wellness Counseling and Mentoring Center
Deliverance From The Stronghold Of Suicide

This manual is based in over 20 years experience in professional counseling.

kingdomwellnesscenter@gmail.com

kingdomshifters.com

Connect with Taquetta via Facebook or YouTube

CONTENTS

Vision Statement..v

Taquetta Baker, Founder vii

Book Synopsis x

Setting the scene xii

Suicide Defined 2

Suicidal Ideation 3

Reasons For Suicidal Ideation 6

Insights Regarding Suicidal Ideation 9

Suicidal Signs & Symptoms...11

Spiritual Warfare Of Suicidal Ideation 13

Suicide & the Bible..19

The Spirit Of Suicide 24

Suicide & God 30

Assisting A Person With Suicidal Ideation....................38

Self-Care As The Support Person.................................48

Counseling Exploration For Loved ones Of Suicide Victims.......49

Keys To Avoid Surrendering To Suicide........................51

Helping Children & Teens Avoid Suicide 53

Helping Ministers Avoid Suicide 58

VISION STATEMENT

Kingdom Wellness offers a revolutionary theory of bridging mental and physical health with biblical truths, faith-based counseling, deliverance and healing principles. This is a holistic ideology of the total person – body, soul (mind, will, emotions), and spirit becoming one.

Kingdom Wellness

Mental & Physical

Spiritual Well-

"Psychological theories are valuable for guiding practice in education, mental health, business, and other domains. They provide answers to intrinsically interesting questions concerning many kinds of thinking including perception, emotion, learning, and problem-solving."

TAQUETTA BAKER, FOUNDER

A trailblazer of deliverance, healing, wellness, fine arts, warfare, and apostolic reform, Taquetta knows the lifelong journey of processing and evolving effectively and successfully. She understands being strengthened by the pain that life can bring while embracing the joy and trials of unexpected SHIFTS in her destiny journey. Taquetta has transformed her experiences to establish a legacy of pioneering strategic godly visions, and raising up fearlessly leaders for his glory.

Taquetta Baker is the founder of Kingdom Shifters Ministries (KSM), Kingdom Shifters Empowerment Church, and Kingdom Wellness Counseling and Mentoring Center. She has authored over 38 books and two prayer CD's. Taquetta has a Doctorate in Ministry, a Master's Degree in Community Counseling with an emphasis on Marriage, Children and Family Counseling, a Bachelor's Degree in Psychology and Associates Degree in Business Administration. Taquetta has a Therapon Belief Therapist Certification from the Therapon Institute, which provides faith-based counseling and ministry training.

Taquetta serves in the mental health field as a Behavioral Consultant. She enjoys working with individuals and families who experience a broad range of psychological, emotional, social, relational, and spiritual challenges. Her outreach demonstrates cultural agility across a spectrum of ages, ethnicities, and socio-economic backgrounds. She is committed to empowering others with launching ministries, businesses, and books. She provides mentoring, counseling and vision launching through her Kingdom Wellness Counseling and Mentoring Center. With over 22 years of faith-based and professional counseling experience, her reputation is one who transforms lives and families through balancing biblical principles with applicable tools and strategies.

Taquetta serves on the Board of Directors for New Day Community Ministries, Inc. and is a graduate of the Eagles Dance Institute under Dr. Pamela Hardy with a license in liturgical dance. Before pioneering her own ministry, Taquetta was a dedicated member of Christ Temple Global Ministries for 14 years. She served pioneered Shekinah Expressions dance ministry and served in the role of prophet, teacher, presbytery board member, and overseer of the Altar Workers Ministry. Taquetta receives mentoring and ministry covering from Bishop Jackie Green, Founder of JGM-National Prayer Life Institute (Phoenix, AZ), and was ordained as an Apostle on June 7, 2014.

The Bible is full of stories that are centered around digging or receiving from wells which represent stability and deep places of renewal. Taquetta flows through the spiritual wells of warfare, worship, counseling and deliverance. Taquetta's mantle is an apostolic directive of judging and establishing God's kingdom in people, ministries, communities, and regions. Taquetta travels in foreign missions and throughout the United States. She has mentored and established dance teams, altar workers, counseling programs, and deliverance and prophetic ministries. Taquetta ministers in the areas of fine arts, systems of prayer, fivefold ministry, deliverance, healing, miracles, atmospheric worship, and counseling. Her mission is to empower and train others to identify and embrace their destiny.

Shift!

BOOK SYNOPSIS

Life stressors can ensue suicidal thoughts regardless of age, race, gender, economic status or position. This book is designed to provide insight on how suicidal ideation and the spirit of suicide operation, how to be proactive in dismantling suicidal ideation, and how to minister to persons and their loved ones regarding suicidal ideation and suicide.

Deliverance from the Stronghold of Suicide

Kingdomwellnesscenter@gmail.com
www.kingdomshifters.com
Connect with Taquetta via Facebook or YouTube

SETTING THE SCENE
Testimony of Dr. Kathy Williams

The first time I attempted suicide, I was 15 years old. I was in a place where I thought I couldn't do anything right. I was convinced that I was a disappointment to my parents. I was carrying secret shame from a sexual molestation that it seemed everyone BUT my parents and family knew about. I took a handful of pills and laid down on my bed expecting to die in my sleep. When I woke up, my first thought was, "Darn! I tried to kill myself because I can't do anything right, and I can't even do this right!" My second attempt at suicide came at the age of 18 while in an extremely abusive relationship. I was depressed and in despair and felt I had nowhere to turn. I crawled into a closet and sat there with a razor blade trying to figure out how to cut my wrists. It seemed like death was the only way to make the pain stop. As I sat in that darkened closet with tears running down my face, I had this epiphany, "Wait a minute! I'm not even married to this guy! Why am I letting him have this much power?" I crawled into that closet beaten and defeated, but I walked out of that closet with a fighting spirit. The abuse didn't totally stop, but I left that relationship when I was 19 years old.

There have been many points in my life where I didn't feel good enough and suicidal thoughts crossed my mind. After having four children and circumstances feeling like the devil dropped a hand grenade into our family, I once again became suicidal. I drove to a river with the intention of driving into the water and drowning. I was convinced that I had so miserably failed my children that they would be better off without me. Parents are supposed to protect their children, and can I tell you that being a believer who fasted and prayed made me carry an even heavier burden? Why didn't I hear God? Had He tried to warn me or tell me, and I wasn't prayerful enough? Should I have fasted more? Should I have read the Word more? Why wasn't

I enough? In the church, there is an expression about God protecting us from dangers seen and unseen. Sometimes those unseen dangers are what is stirring in our hearts and minds. We can't use any of our five sense to experience despair, but it is as real as eating a sandwich.

Life has taught me a few things about suicide. Life has taught me if a person has ever been suicidal, that the thought will simply pop up as an option. It can be dismissed as easily as any other thought, but the risk begins when we rehearse the idea. Have you noted the recurring thought in my experiences? *I'm not good enough. I don't fit in with anyone around me. I am ashamed of me.* I have had no other suicide attempts, but I have definitely had suicidal thoughts. May I share the most recent with you? I completed a 7-year doctoral program in 3 years. I had straight A's. My reviewing professors said my final doctoral project was a masterpiece. Over and over, people called me a genius and said the world needs to hear my voice. During tha time, I was serving as a full-time chaplain in a men's prison and teaching college classes as adjunct faculty. I was teaching for the Billy Graham Intitute at their annual conference. I had multiple awards and plaques hanging on the wall of my office. While polishing my final doctoral project, I experienced multiple thoughts of suicide. The root of my thoughts centered around, "What if I can't live up to what people think of me?"

Let me summarize by sharing this thought. Think of the devil as a trickster. He is a defeated enemy. Ultimately, the devil hates God but has no power to go against God. We already know what happened the one time he tried that stunt! Luke 10:18 records Jesus saying that Satan fell like lightning from heaven. Who can the devil attack? US!!! When a person becomes suicidal, it is a sign that everything else the devil has tried to wreck your destiny has failed. He is like a magician who has already run through all of his tricks, and the audience still isn't laughing. As a final effort, he reaches way down to the bottom of the bag to pull out the final stunt. Perhaps if you have ever struggled with suicide, it is simply the flip side of the coin that holds valuable destiny for you. This book is going to be like holding a mirror so that you can see the details of what takes place in your struggle. I am exited for you to read and see yourself and find some relief and a release. You are greater than a trick bag! You are purposed for destiny! Decreeing your breakthrough as the revelation Dr. Taquetta Baker shares in this book, SHIFTS you into powerful insight that annihilates the stronghold of suicidal ideation and suicide.

Dr. Kathy E. Williams
Founder of New Day Ministries
Muncie, Indiana

SUICIDE DEFINED

Suicide is:

The conscious and self-absorbed stronghold of stress, distress, destitution, and hopelessness where the person deems death as the solution of relief to their problems.

The conscious and self-absorbed act of killing oneself where a needy or unhappy person deems death as the best solution to their problems.

Suicide Is NOT A Coping Mechanism!

Suicide is **NOT** a coping mechanism as it is a finite solution. Coping mechanisms are tools and strategies to help a person maneuver through a situation, experience, or moment in time. Many strive to end their pain with a finite solution that yields no tomorrow.

SUICIDE YIELDS NO TOMORROW!

SUICIDE YIELDS NO TOMORROW!

THERE IS ONLY THE ETERNITY AFTER SUICIDE!

SUICIDAL IDEATION

Suicidal ideation is the psychological stress, obsession, ideology of entertaining and pondering on thoughts and plans regarding suicide. Suicidal thoughts often come to a person in the form of hopelessness, helplessness, despair, desperation, confusion, and depression. These thoughts can range from a detailed plan to a fleeting consideration, yet does not include the final act of suicide.

Suicidal thoughts can feel like a WAR is occurring in the:

Mind = Thoughts

Heart = Emotions

Soul = Innerman

Body = Physically Oppressed Or Possessed By Gloom, Despair, Death

The person is literally at war between:

- Death and Life
- Flesh and Spirit
- Destitution and Reality
- Lies and Truth
- Law of Satan Versus Law of God

> ***Romans 7:23*** *But I see another law in my members, warring against the law of my mind, and bringing me into captivity to the law of sin which is in my members.*

3

A law is anything that has been established as rule, custom, law, command.

The unhealthy-ungodly law has exalted itself above:

- ✓ The knowledge of God.

- ✓ The truth concerning the person's value and purpose in life.

- ✓ The truth of the person's identity and destiny with God.

- ✓ The God himself as now the person believes they have a right to chose whether they should live or die when this is God's position in our lives.

> *2Corinthians 10:5 Casting down imaginations, and every high thing that exalteth itself against the knowledge of God, and bringing into captivity every thought to the obedience of Christ.*

> *The Amplified Bible These weapons can break down every proud argument against God and every wall that can be built to keep men from finding him. With these weapons I can capture rebels and bring them back to God and change them into men whose hearts' desire is obedience to Christ.*

> *The Living Bible These weapons can break down every proud argument against God and every wall that can be built to keep men from finding him. With these weapons I can capture rebels and bring them back to God and change them into men whose hearts' desire is obedience to Christ.*

High thing is *hypsōma* in Greek and means:
1. an elevated place or thing
2. height, i.e. (abstractly) altitude, or (by implication) a barrier (figuratively)
3. high thing, elevated thing, height of space elevated structure, i.e. barrier, rampart, bulwark

The life challenge and the suicidal ideation has exalted itself as law and become a proud argument appearing as a fact and a necessary decision in the person's life.

This is where suicide SHIFTS to being a stronghold that controls the person's will to act on this unhealthy, ungodly law.

DECREEING EVERY UNHEALTHY – UNGODLY LAW IS CAST DOWN RIGHT NOW IN JESUS NAME!

SHIFT!

REASONS FOR SUICIDAL IDEATION

≈ Feeling unfulfilled with life.

≈ Surviving rather than thriving in life.

≈ Overwhelmed by life changes, especially drastic changes that alter one's lifestyle and/or perception of life or self.

≈ A mental illness where suicidal thoughts are part of the symptoms of that illness.

≈ Generational curse and patterns where suicide, self sabotage and/or mental illness is rooted in the family line, or perceived or used as a means to an end.

≈ Relationships with persons who have committed suicide. This opens a door to it being viewed as a solution.

≈ Depression and/or stress due to stressful or traumatic life experiences.

≈ Cycles of depression related to the times, seasons, and climate. Many people become depressed and suicidal in the winter months, around holidays, or at specific times of the year when challenging unresolved experiences have occurred, e.g. death of a loved one, rape, molestation, car accident, physical abuse, violence, terrorism, slavery, sex trafficking, bullying, robbery, kidnapping, lost job, relationship ending, hardship.

≈ A need for love, belonging, a sense of self-worth.

≈ Lack of family support or family enmeshment; unhealthy and inordinate boundaries.

- ≈ Isolation, loneliness, abandoned, rejected.
- ≈ Substance abuse with legal or illegal substances.
- ≈ Certain medications can have side effects of suicidal ideation.
- ≈ School issues, e.g. grades, bullying, disciplinary issues, peer issues.
- ≈ Job issues, e.g. work stress, burnout, overworked, underpaid, unhealthy work environment, hating job, not opportunity for advancement.
- ≈ Financial hardship - sudden or ongoing financial hardship.
- ≈ Poverty, poverty mindset, an onset of poverty.
- ≈ Famine, plagues, pandemics.
- ≈ Ministry challenges, including but not limited to burned out, overburdened with ministry obligations, lack of team assistance, minimal to no ministry support, unhealthy or false perception regarding what it means to be a ministry leader, lack of balance concerning ministry duties, financial hardship, psychological warfare, persecution, fear of failing people and/or God, pressures to succeed, failure to take respite and sabbaticals, unresolved soul issues, sin struggles, false perception regarding self-care and mental health.
- ≈ Imprisonment or trouble with law enforcement. (Proven to be mot at-risk within the first 24 hours of incarceration.)
- ≈ Prone to irresponsible, unhealthy, erratic, impulsive behaviors.
- ≈ For attention, provoke a response from others, retaliate or punish others.

≈ To get a rise out of someone or incite drama.

≈ To instill fear, control, or manipulation in others.

≈ To avoid consequences or to obtain one's needs and desires from others.

≈ To escape consequences, responsibilities, and situations, where follow through and accountability is needed.

≈ Being deprived of sleep and/or rest.

≈ Reoccurrences of suicidal thoughts or suicidal experiences.

≈ Belief systems and experiences that reject people because of race, class, gender, sexual orientation.

≈ Belief systems that view suicide as as an act of mortar.

≈ Territorial or spiritual warfare from the demonic spirits that govern a region, a community, or destiny killing spirits that want to stifle or murder a person's fate

≈ Witchcraft and bewitching released through word curses, spells, hexes, vexes, incantations.

INSIGHTS REGARDING SUICIDAL IDEATION

Many people who have suicidal thoughts do not act on them; however, each situation should be taken seriously.

Even if a person is using suicide for attention seeking their comments should not be taken lightly. Suicidal ideation is still on their mind and is part of how they are getting their need for love and value met. These can the most dangerous persons as they have the potential to make abrupt decisions regarding suicide - decisions that cannot be undone regardless to the fact that it was just to provoke a response or attention for someone. It is important to get such persons professional help where they can deal with identity issues, unresolved life experiences, learn healthy coping skills, and ways to get their needs for love and value met in a healthy manner.

Most people experience suicidal ideation at some point in their lives. People have low points in their lives. Thoughts of not wanting to live and wishing they were dead start to plague their mind, heart, and soul.

Some people who commit suicide show no signs or symptoms. They live one way in public and another in their private thoughts or isolated settings, while acting upon their internal ideation, leaving people around them shocked that they wanted to take their lives.

TV shows have helped to desensitize suicide and make it a coping mechanism or a means to an end. Many TV shows have people killing themselves to avoid jail, the consequences of their actions, as a means to deal with trying or hopeless situations, and for shock value. This sensationalism and constant visualization has given teens and children ideas and ways to kill themselves

SUICIDAL SIGNS & SYMPTOMS

From Medicalnewstoday.com

- Feeling or appearing to feel trapped or hopeless
- Feeling intolerable emotional pain
- Having or appearing to have an abnormal preoccupation with violence, dying, or death
- Having mood swings, either happy or sad
- Talking about revenge, guilt, or shame
- Being agitated, or in a heightened state of anxiety
- Experiencing changes in personality, routine, or sleeping patterns
- Consuming drugs or more alcohol than usual, or starting drinking when they had not previously done so
- Engaging in risky behavior, such as driving carelessly or taking drugs
- Getting their affairs in order and giving things away
- Getting hold of a gun, medications, or substances that could end a life
- Experiencing depression, panic attacks, impaired concentration
- Increased isolation
- Talking about being a burden to others
- Psychomotor agitation, such as pacing around a room, wringing one's hands, and removing items of clothing and putting them back on
- Saying goodbye to others as if it were the last time

- Seeming to be unable to experience pleasurable emotions from normally pleasurable life events such as eating, exercise, social interaction, or sex
- Severe remorse and self criticism
- Talking about suicide or dying, expressing regret about being alive or ever having been born

SPIRITUAL WARFARE OF SUICIDAL IDEATION

Sometimes suicidal thoughts come in the form of psychological and mental warfare to get a person off balance when all is going well in the person's life, or when a person is at a significant peak of breakthrough in their life. These thoughts may be coming from outside demonic chatter being released on the frequencies and airways within the person's sphere of influence. This chatter can be coming from:

≈ Witches, warlocks, wicked people, witchcraft dabblers, releasing spells, hexes, and incantations against the person.

- o ***Leviticus 19:31*** *Regard not them that have familiar spirits, neither seek after wizards, to be defiled by them: I [am] the LORD your God.*
- o ***Leviticus 20:6*** *And the soul that turneth after such as have familiar spirits, and after wizards, to go a whoring after them, I will even set my face against that soul, and will cut him off from among his people.*
- o ***Deuteronomy 18:10-11 New International Bible*** *Let no one be found among you... who practices divination or sorcery, interprets omens, engages in witchcraft, or cast spells, or who is a medium or spiritist.*
- o ***Micah 5:10-12 New International Bible*** *In that day," declares the Lord, "I will destroy your horses from among you and demolish your chariots. I will destroy the cities of your land and tear down all your*

strongholds. I will destroy your witchcraft and you will no longer cast spells.

o ***Isaiah 8:19-22 New International Bible*** *When someone tells you to consult mediums and spiritists, who whisper and mutter, should not a people inquire of their God? Why consult the dead on behalf of the living? Consult God's instruction and the testimony of warning. If anyone does not speak according to this word, they have no light of dawn. Distressed and hungry, they will roam through the land; when they are famished, they will become enraged and, looking upward, will curse their king and their God. Then they will look toward the earth and see only distress and darkness and fearful gloom, and they will be thrust into utter darkness.*

o ***Revelations 18:23*** *The light of a lamp will never shine in you again. The voice of bridegroom and bride will never be heard in you again. Your merchants were the world's important people. By your magic spell all the nations were led astray.*

≈ Uninformed people, contentious people, speaking releasing negative words, curse words, and word curses, against the person.

14

- *Numbers 22:12* But God said to Balaam, "Do not go with them. You must not put a curse on those people, because they are blessed."
- *Psalm 109:17 English Standard Bible* He loved to curse; let curses come upon him! He did not delight in blessing; may it be far from him!
- *Proverbs 26:2* Like a fluttering sparrow or a darting swallow, an undeserved curse does not come to rest.
- *Ecclesiastes 10:20* Curse not the king, no not in your thought; and curse not the rich in your bedchamber: for a bird of the air shall carry the voice, and that which has wings shall tell the matter.
- *James 3:9-10 English Standard Bible* With it we bless our Lord and Father, and with it we curse people who are made in the likeness of God. From the same mouth come blessing and cursing. My brothers, these things ought not to be so.
- *James 3:8-11 New International Bible* But no human being can tame the tongue. It is a restless evil, full of deadly poision. Out of the tongue we praise our Lord and Father, and with it we curse human beings, who have been made in God's likeness. Out of the same mouth come praise and cursing. My brothers and sisters, this should not be. Can both fresh water and salt water flow from the same spring?

- o *Philippians 4:8 Finally, brothers and sisters, whatever is true, whatever is noble, whatever is right, whatever is pure, whatever is lovely, whatever is admirable—if anything is excellent or praiseworthy—think about such things.*

- ≈ Principalities, powers, and territorial spirits that govern the regions, frequencies, atmospheres, the person is privy too.
  - o *Ephesians 6:12 For we wrestle not against flesh and blood, but against principalities, against powers, against the rulers of the darkness of this world, against spiritual wickedness in high places.*

These demonic spirits and systems release words and curses but also use the words and curses that are released on the airways about the person as fiery darts against that person. This is the reason the word tells us to watch what we speak as there is life and death in the power of the tongue (*Proverbs 18:21*) and to guard our hear with diligence as out of it flows the issues of life (*Proverbs 4:23*). When we are not watchful of our words and heart, we can speak and release words that can bind and become a stronghold in our lives and the lives of others.

The more people yield to these attacks, the impacts of the attacks override the person's identity, while stealing their strength, confidence, focus, and progress. As the person dwells and meditates on these thoughts, it opens the door for the spirit of suicide to start pestering and talking to the person, encouraging them to take their life. By then, the person is usually physically isolated and alone, or despite not being alone, they are living inside their emotions and mind, while being bombarded by this spirit. They start to believe that killing themselves is the only option and solution, thus taking their life.

Some people may never attempt suicide, but due to entertaining suicidal thoughts, they live life reaping the following dreadful consequences:

- ≈ Bitterness of heart and soul
- ≈ Self-hatred
- ≈ Dread for life
- ≈ Pessimism
- ≈ Cynical
- ≈ Loneliness
- ≈ Isolation
- ≈ Misery
- ≈ Relationship challenges and deeper loneliness because people do not want to be around a downer
- ≈ Difficulty connecting to others due to fear, mistrust, and victim mentality that comes with suicidal ideation
- ≈ Depression

Such people tend to never see the good in life and when good occurs, they fear, speak, and even create challenges to prove that death is the best option for them. Often such people are oppressed by a spirit of suicide to which we will discuss next.

SUICIDE & THE BIBLE

Suicide is viewed as a sin because it is an unauthorized taking of one's life (*Exodus 20:17*). This does not necessarily means it is unpardonable, as the only sin listed as unpardonable is blaspheme against the Holy Spirit.

> *Mark 3:28-29 Verily I say unto you, All sins shall be forgiven unto the sons of men, and blasphemies wherewith soever they shall blaspheme: But he that shall blaspheme against the Holy Ghost hath never forgiveness, but is in danger of eternal damnation.*

Though suicide is not listed as unpardonable, we do not know if there is an ability to repent after death. When a person is in a suicidal state, they are typically not communing with God. They have SHIFTED out of communing with him, where they can hear truth about their value, and receive encouragement to live and overcome in life. Since we do not know how God will view a person in such a state and whether he will grant grace, it is best to state that only God knows whether a person goes to heaven or hell once committing suicide. I would contend that it is best not to put oneself in this position and risk hell being one's eternal portion.

In *Judges 9:53-54*, we find wicked, prideful, Abimelech committing suicide, while persuading his armorbearer to help. He did not want it to be said that a woman had cracked his skull, causing his death.

In *Judges 16:29-30*, Samson sacrificed his life in a military act to fulfill his destiny of destroying the philistines. It is unclear if God viewed this as suicide or an heroic mission. Only God knows his eternal destiny and whether he was received in heaven or will spend eternity in hell.

In *1Samuel 31:4*, King Saul fell on his own sword to prevent capture and any further consequences that would have come because of his actions against David and his army.

In *2Samuel 17:23*, Ahithophel hung himself, after recognizing that his counsel to Absalom regarding how to pursue and kill David was not utilized.

In *1Kings 16:16-18*, Zimri set himself afire in the king's house after Omri, the Israeli army's commander cam against him in the city of Tirzah. He actually had taken the throne by killing King Asa of Judah, subsequently reigning over the city of Tirzah.

In *Jonah 1:11-15*, Jonah asked to be thrown overboard because he did not want those on the boat to ensure judgment that he knew was due to him running from the calling of the Lord. Even as he was thrown overboard, he was swallowed up in great fish rather than drowning as this was more of a sacrifice than wanting to die. Jonah was running from what God was telling him to do. It is uncertain whether we could call his actions suicidal; however, he knew with certainty that being thrown into the sea would result in death.

In *Matthew 27:3-10*, Judas a disciple of Jesus hung himself after recognizing that his acts towards Jesus was betrayal.

In *Acts 16:27-30*, Paul prevented the jailer from killing himself. The jailer though Paul and Silas had escaped and drew his sword to kill himself, rather than face the consequences that would have come had they escaped. The jailer immediately saw the prison doors opening after praise and worship as a supernatural act, along with the fact that Paul and Silas did not use it to escape that he asked "what must I do to be saved?" He drew to God for salvation and eternal life, which is what every person should do.

In each of these situations, the person was either not living for God or was out of alignment with him. We can probably suppose their fate, but for some, only God knows. In that manner, I contend, it is best not to place oneself in this situation. Such a decision leaves a person's love ones in an agonizing state of trauma. They are left with the question, "Why?" The pain and torment that those who are left behind go through is not worth yielding one's life to suicide. While relieving one's pain through a decision of death, you have relinquish unfathomable pain on those who have to live with the memory of your decision.

There are several others in the Bible who contemplated death has a means to ending their difficult life. I will list a few here and discuss more later when examining deliverance from suicidal ideation.

In *Numbers 11:14-15*, Moses was burdened by the weight of carrying and leading the people. He asked God for favor to assist with his burden and death if God did not want to provide it. God immediately provided strategy of appointing elders to assist him with his duties.

In the book of Job, we find God allowing Satan to test him by taking away his wealth and family. Job was so grieved by the experience that in *Job 3:11*, he asked "Why did I not die at birth, come out from the womb and expire?" He and God went through various explorations concerning his life, what areas needed to be transformed in him, how he should have handled the testing, and how he needed to SHIFT from just works of worship and religious acts, into a greater personal lifestyle relationship journey with the Lord. It was no doubt that even in needing this SHIFT, Job was faithful and loved the Lord. God restored unto him greater than what was lost in this test.

In *Jeremiah 20:14*, Jeremiah acknowledge that his prophetic calling was so overwhelming until he cursed the day of his birth. He could not fathom the reason God would create him for such a challenging calling. God; however, strengthened him and he was able to endure the persecution and thorn of his calling even though no one ever regarding his prophetic utterances. We learn from him that our calling is not about how others respond or how we perceive it, but about whether we do and fulfill the calling of God on our lives.

THE SPIRIT OF SUICIDE

When people are constantly plagued with suicidal thoughts and are repeatedly considering suicide, they may be encountering a demonic spirit of suicide that is assigned to steal their destiny. This is called a destiny killing spirit. It comes to abort a person's life and in this case, cause the person to abort their own life. Demonic spirits track people from birth and gain intel regarding the person's purpose. By creating havoc in the person's life, the intended outcome is that the person will sabotage their own destiny. It is a bold spirit, has no age limit, and will go to great lengths to make the person believe that self-induced death is the best option for them. In an extremist form, the belief becomes hat killing themselves will ensure martyrdom. As the person contemplates this spirit's plot, it opens the doors to thoughts of "how" to commit the act. This is the reason persons of all ages, even little children, succumb to suicide. The spirit itself gives them the plan - sometimes several plans - on how to end their lives.

The DEVIL came to Jesus after he had fasted forty days and forty nights, told him who he was, tried to make him prove who he was, and dared him to throw himself from the top of the temple.

> *Matthew 4:5-6 Then the devil taketh him up into the holy city, and setteth him on a pinnacle of the temple, And saith unto him, If thou be the Son of God, cast thyself down: for it is written, He shall give his angels charge concerning thee: and in their hands they shall bear thee up, lest at any time thou dash thy foot against a stone.*

In *1Kings 19*, we find Prophet Elijah asking God to take his life after being threatened by Queen Jezebel. Queen Jezebel was angry at Prophet Elijah for defeating her prophets in a *"who is the true and living God"* challenge. Prophet Elijah made a spectacle of her, her prophets, their false god, and slaughtered all her prophets. She sent a messenger (word curse of intimidation, control, and hopelessness) to let Prophet Elijah know she was not happy with his actions, and that she was seeking to kill him. He became depressed, frightened, and ran for his life. This curse had him separating from his sphere of influence, his supports, and what could encourage, empower, and speak truth to him. While isolated and on the run, he experienced such despair that he asked the Lord to take his life. This word curse operated as a destiny killing spirit of murder that had Prophet Elijah running to spare his life, yet wanting to take his own life. That is how a destiny killing spirit works. It will have you using the very thing that wants to kill you as a self-defeating weapon where you use it against yourself. **MY LORD!**

> ***1Kings 19:4*** *But he himself went a day's journey into the wilderness, and came and sat down under a juniper tree: and he requested for himself that he might die; and said, It is enough; now, O Lord, take away my life; for I am not better than my fathers.*

This spirit attacks most people at some point in their lives. It is NOT a reflection of the person's character nor a statement that the person has no coping mechanisms or is downtrodden, uneducated, or deprived. Sometimes when it attacks, it can feel like you are already dead, experiencing a measure of death, or that your life has become a living hell, even though you are still alive. David calls this hell on earth, *"the valley of the shadow of death experience."*

> **Psalms 23** *The LORD is my shepherd; I shall not want. He makes me lie down in green pastures. He leads me beside still waters. He restores my soul. He leads me in paths of righteousness for his name's sake. Even though I walk through the valley of the shadow of death, I will fear no evil, for you are with me; your rod and your staff, they comfort me. You prepare a table before me in the presence of my enemies; you anoint my head with oil; my cup overflows. Surely goodness and mercy shall follow me all the days of my life, and I shall dwell in the house of the LORD forever.*

> **The Amplified Bible** *Yes, though I walk through the [deep, sunless] valley of the shadow of death, I will fear or dread no evil, for You are with me; Your rod [to protect] and Your staff [to guide], they comfort me.*

When a shadow comes upon a person, it shields and separates them from light, energy, heat, resources, reality, and proper perception of things. It also hinders the able to discern the correct direction to take, the times, and seasons, due the person being cast under the shade and darkness. This is how the spirit of death works. It causes separation and distorts truth, life, and light. David reveals that at times, his valley experiences felt like his soul had literally entered hell, a place of death, even though he was on earth. As I consider this concept, I believe this is the reason some people believe it is okay to follow through with suicide. Their soul has entered the shadow of death and they believe it is okay to succumb to it.

Psalms 86:13 *For great is thy mercy toward me: and thou hast delivered my soul from the lowest hell.*

Psalms 16:10 *For You will not abandon my soul to Sheol; Nor will You allow Your Holy One to undergo decay.*

Psalms 30:3 *O LORD, You have brought up my soul from Sheol; You have kept me alive, that I would not go down to the pit.*

Psalms 56:13 *For You have delivered my soul from death, Indeed my feet from stumbling, So that I may walk before God In the light of the living.*

Indicators that the soul may be in hell:

1. When the person feels as if they are experiencing or living hell on earth.
2. When the person feels like as if they are dying.
3. When the person wants to die.
4. When the person wants to kill themselves or is having suicidal thoughts.
5. When the person feels extremely hopeless, helpless, lonely, dejected, rejected, and depressed.
6. When the person is dull in their spiritual walk or grieved in their soul such that they are unable to praise and worship God - it feels like a void of praise and worship. There is no desire or will to praise and worship.
7. When the person feels such darkness and oppression that they have literally become sick - afflicted by the very posture their soul has taken.

27

8. When the person feels strapped and seized by their situation or life as if there is no way out.

9. When the person is void of direction, guidance, and exists within a stronghold of darkness and hopelessness.

10. When everything looks dark and gloomy around the person and it is as if everything is dying or not working.

11. When the person feels like they have been exiled. Sometimes the experiences and circumstances can exile the person, or sin issues can cause them to be exiled by God.

12. When the person is experiencing extreme judgment and condemnation that feels like torture or torment. This can be in general or due to unrepented sin.

13. When the person live in extreme sin and no longer are convicted by their lifestyle.

Jesus, Elijah, and David lets us know that God is a deliverer of the shadow of death and any way it tries to kill a person or provokes a person to kill themselves. As we reflect on the scriptures I listed above, David says that God is merciful, near, a keeper, and deliverer. In *Psalms 23*, the word *rod* signifies a weapon of authority, power, government, rulership, royalty, protection, fighting, ruling, walking, correction, septre. *Staff* serves as a pillar of support and guidance. David understood that regardless of his death valley experiences, God had a rod and a staff to comfort him – that there was RELIEF and DELIVERANCE even when his life felt like hell.

From the time God created mankind, the devil has been trying to kill them. God created man such that eternal life would be our portion. The devil seduce man and caused death to enter the earth. Throughout history, the quality and value for life has declined, become desensitized, and demoralized, until it is easy for the shadow of death and the spirit of suicide to increase its attack on people; thus taking people out during challenging and unwanted SHIFTS, transitions, and strategic elevations. Prophet Elijah was at the top of his game – at a height of success – and this spirit came to SHIFT him down. Jesus was at a season of consecration, sanctification, communion, and preparation for elevation. The enemy wanted to SHIFT Jesus down before he could experience the fruit of his labor. Like Jesus, it is important to know one's worth and one's ordained identity. And like Elijah, when a person is faltering in knowing their identity, it is best to commune with God so that he can build them in the truth of who they are. This way the enemy cannot twist one's perception where the person becomes their own demise.

SHIFT! SHIFT RIGHT NOW!

SUICIDE & GOD

David was on point when we he said God was a reliever and deliverer despite his shadow of death experience. His posture helped him find the light in darkness. Jesus is indeed the light in darkness. Jesus' entire purpose was to overthrow death, while providing us with life and that more abundantly. He is what overcomes darkness and produces light in our lives and situations.

> *John 1:5* *The light shines in the darkness, and the darkness has not overcome it.*

> *John 8:12* *When Jesus spoke again to the people, he said, "I am the light of the world. Whoever follows me will never walk in darkness, but will have the light of life.*

> *John 10:10* *The thief cometh not, but for to steal, and to kill, and to destroy: I am come that they might have life, and that they might have it more abundantly.*

One notion I love about Elijah and David is that they talked with God about their suicidal tendencies. They took their thoughts and feelings to the Lord, which enabled him to provide comfort, solution, and breakthrough from their experience. Communing with God and exchanging light for darkness, is an essential key for being delivered from the stronghold of suicide. Communing with God:

≈ Shifts a person out of darkness into the light and life of God.

≈ Shifts a person out of listening to the devil, principalities and powers, and one's own thoughts, and into hearing the voice of God.

30

≈ Shifts a person out of vain imaginations and ideologies that have exalted themselves about the word, knowledge, and truth of God.

≈ Shifts a person out of the false identity that the enemy is striving to get the person to believe, into the true identity of God.

≈ Shifts a person out of hopelessness and helplessness, into faith and encouragement of God.

Sometimes a person is able to commune with God without assistance and receive a SHIFT into the light and life of God. And other times they may need the intervention, support, and counsel of others to aide them in receiving their deliverance. Either way, it is important to note that God desires a person to thrive in life, while it is the devil that kill, steals, and destroys.

> **John 10:10** *The thief comes only to steal and kill and destroy. I came that they may have life and have it abundantly.*

This scriptural revelation is so significant in understanding that suicide is not of God. His purpose was for us to live in eternal life from the beginning. That never changes no matter how difficult life becomes.

We know from Bible stories and revelation that has already been shared, that life can become so challenging that death seems a logical solution. But God's purpose is for us to fulfill our life plan. God's purpose is for us to excel in the will and purpose for our lives. This is the reason he journeys with us as a lifestyle. Apart from him, we are just existing, but with him, we can achieve anything.

> **Psalms 34:17-19 The Amplified Bible** *When the righteous cry for help, the Lord hears, and delivers them out of all their distress and troubles. The Lord is close to those who are of a broken heart and saves such as are crushed with sorrow for sin and are humbly and thoroughly penitent. Many evils confront the [consistently] righteous, but the Lord delivers him out of them all.*

The fall of man SHIFTED humanity toward some trying times throughout the earth, but God is a deliverer. What may appear to crush a person to death is but a light matter to God.

> **Jeremiah 32:27** *Behold, I am the LORD, the God of all flesh: is there any thing too hard for me?*

> **Matthew 19:26** *But Jesus looked at them and said, "With man this is impossible, but with God all things are possible.*

A person can be:
- ✓ Encouraged during a time of destitution and hopelessness
- ✓ Assisted with resolving problems that caused the suicidal thoughts
- ✓ Fulfilled in the desires and needs to improve one's life and emotional well being

But without continual communing with God, as soon as another life challenge occur, suicidal ideation will find its way back into the person's life. This is the reason establishing relationship with God and being transformation in seeking him as a lifestyle is sufficient.

> **Deuteronomy 31:8** *And the LORD, he [it is] that doth go before thee; he will be with thee, he will not fail thee, neither forsake thee: fear not, neither be dismayed.*

> **Isaiah 41:10-13** *Fear thou not; for I [am] with thee: be not dismayed; for I [am] thy God: I will strengthen thee; yea, I will help thee; yea, I will uphold thee with the right hand of my righteousness.*

> **Isaiah 55:6-7** *Seek the Lord while He may be found; Call upon Him while He is near. Let the wicked forsake his way And the unrighteous man his thoughts; And let him return to the Lord, And He will have compassion on him, And to our God, For He will abundantly pardon.*

> **Psalms 55:22** *Cast thy burden upon the LORD, and he shall sustain thee: he shall never suffer the righteous to be moved.*

> **Psalms 65:4** *How blessed is the one whom You choose and bring near to You to dwell in Your courts. We will be satisfied with the goodness of Your house, your holy temple.*

> **Psalms 96:8** *Ascribe to the Lord the glory of His name; Bring an offering and come into His courts.*

> **Psalms 100:2-4** *Serve the Lord with gladness; Come before Him with joyful singing. Know that the Lord Himself is God; It is He who has made us, and not we ourselves; We are His people and the sheep of His pasture. Enter His gates with thanksgiving and His courts with praise. Give thanks to Him, bless His name.*

> **Psalms 145:18** *The Lord is near to all who call upon Him, To all who call upon Him in truth.*

Jeremiah 3:22 *"Return, O faithless sons, I will heal your faithlessness." "Behold, we come to You; For You are the Lord our God.*

Jeremiah 29:13 *You will seek Me and find Me when you search for Me with all your heart.*

Jeremiah 31:3 The Message Bible *GOD told them, "I've never quit loving you and never will. Expect love, love, and more love!*

Matthew 7:7 *Ask, and it shall be given you; seek, and ye shall find; knock, and it shall be opened unto you.*

Romans 8:28 *And we know that for those who love God all things work together for good, for those who are called according to his purpose.*

Romans 8:38-39 *For I am persuaded, that neither death, nor life, nor angels, nor principalities, nor powers, nor things present, nor things to come, nor height, nor depth, nor any other creature, shall be able to separate us from the love of God, which is in Christ Jesus our Lord.*

Hebrews 4:16 *Let us therefore come boldly unto the throne of grace, that we may obtain mercy, and find grace to help in time of need.*

1Peter 5:7 *Casting all your care upon him; for he careth for you.*

Philippians 4:6-7 *Be careful for nothing; but in every thing by prayer and supplication with thanksgiving let your requests be made known unto God. And the peace of God, which passeth all understanding, shall keep your hearts and minds through Christ Jesus.*

Connecting with God and adhering to what he said is what saved those in the Bible who considered death as an option, and this is what will save a person today.

The truth is, all of mankind is fighting for their right to have life, and to live in the fullness of salvation with God.

> *Matthew 11:12 And from the days of John the Baptist until now the kingdom of heaven suffereth violence, and the violent take it by force.*

> *1Timothy 6:12 Fight the good fight of the faith. Take hold of the eternal life to which you were called and about which you made the good confession in the presence of many witnesses.*

This truth needs to be taught from birth so that a person can be clear about the trials that can come with life and how to overcome them. This also needs to be taught to believers so they can have a realistic understanding of their walk and how to effectively journey with God through the good and bad times.

A person has to want relationship with God to receive restoration of fellowship with him. When they are resistant, continual intercession will be required to break the spirit of suicide from the person. They also may be oppressed with the spirit of unbelief and doubt. Often intercession will have to be done apart from the person as sometimes it will agitate the spirit/s that are oppressing them. But if they are open to it, then pray and intercede where they can hear, partake, and engage in the prayers that are being prayed.

Many people who have yielded to suicidal thoughts do not feel love, safe, valued, or wanted. Helping to dismantle these lies are key to their deliverance. They need to not just know that God is loves them, protects them, honors them, needs them, wants them, they need to be reconnected with these truths. As the person is SHIFTING into communing with God, provide the person with tasks and activities that fills them with these truths. These can include:

- ≈ Journaling or verbally sharing their thoughts and feelings with God, and waiting in his presence for him to speak.
- ≈ Praising, worshipping, and soaking in the presence of the Lord.
- ≈ Soaking the person in the fruit of the spirit, and creating situations where they feel love, valued, honored, safe.
- ≈ Providing scriptures related to life or the person's situation and having them meditate on them.
- ≈ Mature qualified ministers, completing inner healing and deliverance sessions with the person. Often times, there is an underlying root that caused suicide to be a consideration. Spending time counseling, praying, delivering, and cleansing a person of root issues can assist with breaking the powers of suicide.
- ≈ Seek God for revelation on how to assist the person with resolving their life challenges. Encourage them to do the same. Implement what God says. Offer support and assistance as the person processes through the situation. Be mindful that even

though you are their for the person, that they are leaning on God and not seeing you as God. Do not fix them or work them like a project. Draw them to God and allow him to perfect his will and purpose in them.

≈ Teaching the person how to have a relationship with God is vital to breaking the powers of suicide and dismantling future challenges in this area.

Though someone can be delivered from the suicidal ideation or the spirit of suicide instantly, I recommend a sufficient time of follow up support and accountability to ensure they are consistently cdrawing nigh to God and implementing the suggestions to maintain their breakthrough. I also suggest having the person pursue ongoing professional Christian counseling and psychiatric services to further assess and deal with mental health and unresolved issues, to provide a process to wellness, and to learn and utilize maintenance tools to wholeness.

ASSISTING A PERSON WITH SUICIDAL IDEATION

Suicide Hotline - It is always in order to call the suicidal hotline for guidance when dealing with someone who is displaying suicidal ideation. They can assist with how to handle the situation and provide insight on whether contacting the authorities is necessary. The person that is suicidal will mostly likely not want you to call. As the person who is intervening, you should decide if this an appropriate call to make. It is always better to be safe than to live in regret. The confidential National Suicide Prevention Lifeline can be reached toll-free at   1-800-273-TALK(8255), 24 hours a day, 7 days a week.

Remain Calm – Try not to panic if at all possible. Also do not take on the perception that you are now responsible for the person. Though you want to make every effort to intervene, the person still has freewill. Give your best effort and regardless the outcome, life is their decision to make.

Express Concern – Do not feel like you have to say everything perfectly or even know what to say. Expressing and showing concern is the best gift you can give the person.

Listen Attentively & Be Discerning – Be mindful to listen and allow the person to express their thoughts and feelings without interruption. Do not go into fixer mode. Focus on listening and striving to hear

38

what the person is saying and what the spirit of God is telling you regarding what is really occurring with the person. As what, when, how questions rather than yes or no questions, closed ended questions that only result in one or two word answers or why questions as they put a person on the defense. Do not be intimidated by silence. Allow time for the person to answer. Pray silently for God to speak to the person, and for them to receive a release of their burdens even as they are sharing. Examine the person's facial expressions, body language, mood, mood swings, and thought processing. What they are not saying is exuding just as much insight to what they need to be conveying as what they are sharing. Only lend a solution as God leads. Otherwise just remain present with the person until you have direction on what solutions to offer.

Avoid Judgments & Dictatorship Behavior – Allow the person to express whatever thoughts or feelings they are having, especially the negative ones. Allow them to release them as this also releases the grip of the suicidal ideation and the oppression of suicide. Do not express judgment regarding what the person is sharing or try to dictate to them how they should feel. Do not get into arguments about suicide being wrong and definitely do not get into religious debates regarding it. Do not try to make the person consider others by discussing how their actions will impact their loved ones. This will cause the person to defend their perceptions. It also makes them feel like all their life decisions are about others rather than themselves. This will strength the consideration of suicide and further justify their reasons for killing themselves.

Provide Sympathy & Support - Express sympathy and regard for their emotions and perceptions. Keep asking them to explain what they are sharing further. You can also ask them if there is anything else they would like to share. Sometimes people hearing themselves, causes them to ponder their own behavior and need for change. It also can spark wisdom and alternative realistic solutions to a situation. This also creates a safe environment where the person feels loved, valued, secure and that they can be real in how they truly feel. The more these feelings are affirmed, the more optimism for life manifests.

Regard The Person's Perspective – Do not take the thoughts and feelings that the person is sharing lightly. Especially those related to hopelessness, dread, pain, heartache, and death. Keep listening and expressing and demonstrating concerning.

Offer Hope & Prayer – Instead of automatically expressing hope or praying, ask the person if you can share your thoughts and feelings concerning what they have shared and/or if you can pray with them. Allowing them to invite and agree with you being part of their moment, increases the love, consideration and safety they need to feel. It also makes them feel in control of their choices and of the situation. This is key because often considering suicide is about want to feel in control or have some control over what the person is experiencing.

Also if they are dealing with a spirit of suicide, this spirit is controlling. This spirit will want to control how to engage the person. If you appear as if you are fixing the person or abrasively interjecting your presence and perception upon the person, the spirit of suicide will cause the person to become guarded, defensive and even secluded. The person agreeing to allow you to be part of the situation, dismantles this spirit and gives you an opportunity to present hope, strength, encouragement, and God into the situation.

How Ensure Hope & Prayer - The suggested steps for assisting someone with suicide needs to be implemented for a time. This will help with the life transformation the person needs to SHIFT into balance and wellness where they can sustain independently. The more they SHIFT, the more life and emotional wellness needs to be the focus rather than focusing on the suicidal ideation itself.

> *Lead The Prayer* - Make sure you lead the prayer and even lead the person in prayer. This is important because it is hard to pray when battling suicidal thoughts. The desire to pray is not there and the person may be battling anger against God. They need to know that sharing their raw heart with God is praying and is how to build relationship. Encourage them to share exactly how they feel and think and then spend time drawing them into the strength of God.

Build Them Up In Identity & Love - Focus encouragement and prayer on building the person up in their identity, in love, in worth, in value, in safety, and protection. It is quite all right to move in and out of encouragement and prayer - checking on the person, asking questions, providing support, encouragement, and processing anything God may be revealing, and then praying some more. This will help to pray patiently, sympathetically, compassionately, strategically and earnestly as you encourage and build them up. This will also help to pray what the person need and without judgment. This time of prayer and processing is not about them recognizing suicide is sinful but that life is worth living. They are learning God's love, Grace, nearness, and how to tread in earnest prayer and pursue God as a lifestyle as they unity in prayer during this time.

God's Hears & Cares - Focus them on understanding that God hears them and is a present help regarding their lives and situations.

> ***Psalms 46:1*** *God is our refuge and strength, a very present help in trouble.*

> ***Psalms 66:17-20*** *I cried unto him with my mouth, and he was extolled with my tongue.*
> *If I regard iniquity (trouble, sorrow) in my heart, the Lord will not hear me: But verily God hath heard me; he hath attended to the voice of my prayer. Blessed be*

42

God, which hath not turned away my prayer, nor his mercy from me.
***1John 5:14-15** And this is the confidence that we have in him, that, if we ask any thing according to his will, he heareth us: And if we know that he hear us, whatsoever we ask, we know that we have the petitions that we desired of him.*

God Understands - Focus them on the revelation that God cares about them, their challenges, and how they feel about life.

> ***John 15:18-19** If the world hate you, ye know that it hated me before it hated you. If ye were of the world, the world would love his own: but because ye are not of the world, but I have chosen you out of the world, therefore the world hateth you.*

> ***Hebrews 4:15** For we do not have a high priest who is unable to empathize with our weaknesses, but we have one who has been tempted in every way, just as we are--yet he did not sin.*

Casting Out Oppressive Spirits - As the person come into enlightenment with understanding that God cares and hears them, break off the powers and oppressions of suicide and cast out any spirits of death, self- sabotage, and suicide. Usually the spirits of depression, heaviness, apathy, helplessness, hopelessness, fatigue/weariness, fear, anxiety, and stress, work with the spirits of suicide. Spend time breaking their powers of oppression and casting them out of the persons life.

When you break the powers of these demonic spirits, you are annihilating the power and authority they have over the person, and every way they imprisoned and control the person. This is important because it breaks the characteristics of how the demonic spirit has intertwined itself in the person's life.

> *Isaiah 58:6 Is not this the fast that I have chosen? to loose the bands of wickedness, to undo the heavy burdens, and to let the oppressed go free, and that ye break every yoke?*

> *Isaiah 61:1 The Spirit of the Lord GOD is upon me; because the LORD hath anointed me to preach good tidings unto the meek; he hath sent me to bind up the brokenhearted, to proclaim liberty to the captives, and the opening of the prison to them that are bound.*

> When you cast spirits out, you bind and loose the person from the bondage of the oppressive spirit. This frees the person from the manifestation of the demonic spirit.

> *Mark 16:17 And these signs will accompany those who believe: in my name they will cast out demons; they will speak in new tongues.*

Peace - Focus on releasing them from hopelessness, depression, anxiety, and fear, and moving into a place where the peace of God overtakes them. Peace calms the storm in and around the person and in their situation.

> *John 14:27 Peace I leave with you, my peace I give unto you: not as the world giveth, give I unto you. Let not your heart be troubled, neither let it be afraid.*

***John 16:33** These things I have spoken unto you, that in me ye might have peace. In the world ye shall have tribulation: but be of good cheer; I have overcome the world.*

Restore Joy Of Salvation - Focus on releasing joy back into the person's life. Do this by asking God to release joy upon the person. Further break spirits of depression, heaviness, and hopelessness that hinders joy from manifesting. Have the person focus on receiving. Do not pressure the person to receive joy. Trust that God is working regardless of their response or what they feel. Joy of salvation is not about a feeling but a spiritual fulfillment that we have through accepting Jesus as our savior. Joy of salvation includes rejoicing in the liberty, deliverance, healing, rescue, protection, covering, safety, welfare, prosperity that being a child of God beings to our lives. As they embrace the truth of what being in salvation with Jesus is, and rejoice in it, joy will restore itself.

While encouraging and processing with the person in this area, search out with them ways joy of salvation was lost and what they can do to restore joy of salvation into their lives. Focus them on things they have control over and explore with them ways to trust, and release to God with the areas they have no control over. He is their savior and has the ultimate authority over all things.

Psalms 30:11 *You have turned for me my mourning into dancing; You have loosed my sackcloth and girded me with gladness.*
Psalms 51:8 *Make me to hear joy and gladness, let the bones which You have broken rejoice.*

Psalms 51:12 *Restore to me the joy of Your salvation and sustain me with a willing spirit.*

Psalms 80:7 *O God of hosts, restore us and cause Your face to shine upon us, and we will be saved.*

Jeremiah 30:19 *And out of them shall proceed thanksgiving and the voice of them that make merry: and I will multiply them, and they shall not be few; I will also glorify them, and they shall not be small.*

The Message Bible *Thanksgivings will pour out of the windows; laughter will spill through the doors. Things will get better and better. Depression days are over. They'll thrive, they'll flourish. The days of contempt will be over.*

Wait For Strategy - For those things where intervention is possible, seek God for a strategy or answer for their situation. Wait for him to speak. Also seek wise counsel and professional assistance as needed. Assist the person in implementing the strategy at hand.

Avoid Promising Confidentiality – Do not agree to keep the person's suicidal thoughts or intentions a secret. If the person ask this of you, let them know that you will make the best decision that ensures their life. If they are insistent with you explaining this comment, just express that you do not want to make a promise that you may not be able to keep, so you digress on making such a promise. When the person is demanding secrecy, it is best to seek a professional for guidance to ensure the safety of the person. I therefore, suggest calling the suicide hotline for insight. They will provide information on how to intervene and can guide you accordingly. This is the most essential advice as the spirit of suicide does not play fair. They love secrecy so they can further plague and oppress the person and draw them into a suicide plan. Give this spirit no room. Your focus is to give the person every ample opportunity to live even if they choose to still take their life. It is best to have an angry person who is upset because you intervened than a dead person because you kept an oath that should have never been made in the first place.

SELF-CARE AS THE SUPPORT PERSON

≈ Be sure to cleanse of any trauma, shock and awe that was experienced from supporting and assisting a suicidal person with deliverance.

≈ Break any powers and spirits of heaviness and depression that may impact you from being around the person or carrying the burden of the person.

≈ Share with God any thoughts and feelings you have regarding the experience and release all responsibilities to the Lord.

≈ Seek wise counsel or a professional counseling if the experience starts to negative impact your emotions and everyday life. It would be beneficial to immediately seek wise counsel or a capable person to process and pray with you to provide support and healing to your own state of mind and wellness.

Ecclesiastes 4:9 Two are better than one; because they have a good reward for their labour.

COUNSELING EXPLORATION FOR LOVED ONES OF SUICIDE VICTIMS

≈ Help them work through the shock, awe, trauma and grief of loosing a loved one.

≈ Help them process any guilt, shame, and condemnation, they maybe experiences surrounding their lost.

≈ Help them process their challenges with the after life of their loved one. Focus them on being at peace that God makes those decisions and he is a just and merciful God. Focus them on trusting him regarding that decision and receiving piece that the decision is his alone.

≈ Help them process and explore coping skills and goals they need to work on to live life without their loved one.

≈ The general stages of grief are as followed:

≈ SHOCK & DENIAL
  ಬ Some people experience trauma depending on the reason for death and the depth of the relationship.
  ಬ Pain & Guilt

- Anger, Scapegoating, & Bargaining

- Depression, Despair, Loneliness

- Reflection, Focusing On Deliverance & Healing

- Reconstruction & Working Through Grief

- Embracing The Healing

- Acceptance & Hope

Understand that the grief process is hard, differs from person to person and is a difficult unexplainable journey to endure. Suicide of a loved one compounds the grief process and requires extreme patience and sympathy when assisting a person through their process. Being a support while allowing a professional counselor to navigate the process is the most ideal decision for the grieved person.

KEYS TO AVOID SURRENDERING TO SUICIDE

- Effective problem-solving – learning how to resolve life challenges in an appropriate manner and utilizing these skills daily, not just when challenges arise.
- Healthy emotional regulation – learning and living through healthy emotional wellness.
- Honoring the need for mental health services – recognizing mental health services as part of living a well and whole life. Receiving counseling and psychiatric services for mental illness and mental instability as necessary; even pursuing counseling seasonally for healthy mental maintainance.
- Learning and living through healthy coping skills and conflict resolution skills.
- Learning healthy relationship skills and living a lifestyle of healthy interaction with others.
- Practicing self-care as a lifestyle so that one's mental, physical, emotional, and personal wellbeing can be balanced.
- Positive and available supports – having healthy mentoring relationships, wise counsel, and trusting relationships that empower life, health living, while offering wisdom and support when towering through life challenges. Journeying with these supports as a lifestyle so that when challenges arise, utilizing them as trusted voices will be easy and viewed as beneficial.
- Confident support seeking – consistently utilizing supports when needed; especially when life becomes challenging; resisting

isolation and allowing life challenges and demonic chatter to withdraw from supports.

- Developing a purpose driven life – living a life of ordained destiny rather than just doing good or engaging in activities and careers just to survive, empowers a sense of self-worth and strength's one's identity.

HELPING CHILDREN & TEENS AVOID SUICIDE

- Build them in their God identity so that people, demons, society, works, activities, and situations won't define them.

- Seek to meet a their needs for self-actualization, esteem, love, belonging, safety, and psysiology, so that they will not compromise or sacrifice their identity to have them met.

- Develop and have real relationships, conversations, and interactions with them that are more than just providing for their needs and desires.

- Keep communication, honest, open, safe, and share personal trials and experiences so that they feel they can discuss any situation be heard and regarded. Be quick to listen and even if punishment is in order, be slow to punish so that they feel safe to share without shutting down, becoming secretive, or rebellious.

- Ask detailed questions to teach them how to express their thoughts and feelings, and how to share their issues, concerns, and challenges in an in-depth manner where they efficiently express and expose what is internally and secretly occurring in their lives. Be mindful to hear and listen to what they are not telling you; ask detailed questions before providing a solution, as sometimes providing quick solutions can cause the them to shut down and be hesitant to share. Focus on being one to help guide them into healthy problem solving and providing a solution than a fixer. They are not projects to fix. They are children and teens who need to be trained and equipped with how to cope and navigate in life.

- Know that children and teens have growing brains. Medical research proves that the final stage of brain development happens between the ages of 18-25. Even though they may appear mature and wise beyond their age in many areas and can possess some key intuitive survival skills, they do not have the mental or intellectual capacity to cope with many stressful issues that they endure, without the guidance of an adult. This is the reason God gave children parents. Do not assume they know how to deal with bullying, peer pressure, peer issues, divorce, a violating experience, etc., just to name a few. There brain is not developed enough to deal with the situation to the manner of which it may be occurring. Do not leave them to deal with it themselves. Journey with them in these experiences. Intervene where necessary. Get the law involved if necessary. Totally remove the child from the situation if necessary. It is better to have people and the child upset than to leave a child in their thoughts to deal with issues, and have them succumb to suicide as a way to handle an experience.

- Never assume suicidal remarks are just for attention or is melodrama. The fact that they would make such a statements reveals that they have entertained such thoughts or have experienced stressed and life challenges to a point of this being a consideration. When hearing such remarks, take responsibility to teach them healthy coping skills and healthy ways to express their thoughts and feelings. Make sure they know that suicide is not a coping mechanism and the consequences of entertaining such remarks and following through with such actions. Set goals and family meetings that promote healthy dialog and healthy coping and support so that the suicidal ideation can be weeded out of their lives and the household in general.

Sometimes they may display classic depressive symptoms and other times when youth are depressed, they may not display any classic depressive symptoms at all. The spirit of suicide uses the nonclassic depressive symptoms as an opportunity to sneak in and steal life from the youth and their loved ones.

- They may appear overelated or joyful so they can hide how they truly feel.
- They may appear emotionless, numb, lifeless, neutral, uninterested, uncaring, or as if they do not have any regard for the consequences or the outcome of the situation, or life in general.
- They may throw themselves into play activities, crafts, sports, video games, to distract their thoughts and feelings, or to give the illusion that all is well with them. They may also do this because they do not know how to cope, express their thoughts or feelings, so they use these activities as a coping mechanism or to just survive in life.
- They may strive to express themselves in drawings, journalings, notes, text messages, social media postings, emails, homework assignments, music, tv shows they seek to watch.
- They may start to give away personal items.

o They may become destructive of their personal items (e.i., toys, clothes,), property, etc.

o They may refuse to care for their grooming and hygiene, become excessive regarding their grooming and hygiene, change their appears and the way they dress.

o They may begin to excessively isolate, spend hours in their room, the bathroom, taking baths, or in their faviorate hideaway place.

o They may neglect chores and become defiant regarding house, school, and community rules and regulations.

o They will SHIFT into survival mode in effort to cope. They are just striving to get through the day and will do whatever necessary in effort to survive. The challenge with this is eventually the breakdown will follow and if no one is their to assist with the breakdown, they are left striving to figure out the next move which is where the spirit of suicide SHIFTS in.

o They will become rebellious, disobedient, defiant, disrespectful, dishonoring, sneaking, secretive, due to overly stressed thoughts and emotions. Parents tend to be so busy striving to assert their right to chastise and receive respect that they miss the opportunities to search out what may be going on with their child. The punishments, whippings, conflict with authority figures, and lack of discernment in recognizing or searching out whether something is wrong, strengthens their hopelessness and the opportunity for the spirit of suicide to operate. This is a time for a parent to become nosey. This is the time for the parent to begin going to the school more and conversing with teachers and counselors, inquiring with peers and any adults or mentors the child or teen is close too, checking their rooms, cell phones, tablets, computers, and social media sits. Many parents often strive to reguard privacy during this time, but this is really the time to step up and be a parent. A child or teen is often striving to express that something is wrong. Parents must remember they are not the child's friend or equal. STEP UP and be a parent.

- o They may become obsessed about death, heaven and/or, God and/or the devil, weapons; they may strive to assure their loved ones that they can live life without them and what that would be like.
- o They may also become beligerant regarding religion and God; not want to attend ministry services or have discussions about God.
- It is essential for parents to consistently pray for their children, and seek God regarding what may be occurring in their lives, so they can be abrest of how to parent and intervene on matters with their children. This will aide in discerning nonclassic symptoms of depression and what maybe occurring behind the scenes.

HELPING MINISTERS AVOID SUICIDE

- Regard and maintain self-care. Ministers need to understand that they cannot give anyone what they do not have themselves as *Matthew 10:8* says "*to freely give as you have received.*" If a minister has not consistently received healing, deliverance, refreshing, breakthrough, training, equipping, revelation, strategy, etc., then it is impossible to give it to someone else. Giving from an empty well cause further depletion of identity. When one's identity is depleted, it is easy for distortion about life and one's perception of self to enter in. Self-care is about esteeming others higher than one's self (*Philippians 2:3*). The foundation of esteeming and pouring into others resides in having a solid foundation of self-care. When a minister has a solid foundationin how they treat themselves, then they can properly pour into the lives of others.

- Learn and utilize emotional wellness, effective problem solving, and healthy coping skills.

- Recognize and utilize mental health - counseling and psychiatric services. Often a minister does not pursuit these services because they are not viewed as part of God's salvation plan for healing. Therefore, mental illness and mental instability is dealt with through general prayer and faith practices that often do not identify or deal with the root issue of mentally ill matters. Also, the ministry of deliverance where demons are confronted is another method for handling these challenges. Yet when this practice does not maintain deliverance, the pursuit of counseling or psychiatric services is not considered or is considered when the situation has become so severe a process to wholeness is needed to dismantle the mental health challenges. Many ministers and people in general find it difficult to weather the process to wholeness and thus tend to abort the process or confound it by cycling into constant behaviors that confound mental health challenges. Suicidal ideation then begins to plague the minister, thus opening the door to this being a viewed as a coping mechanism. Again, suicide is not a coping mechanism. It is a finite solution that cannot be reversed.

- Receive yearly deliverance, inner healing, and counseling services, to deal with the challenges, pains, and warfare of ministry and life in general. It is important to recognize that believers journey with God as a lifestyle. Deliverance is the children's bread (*Matthew 15:21-28, Mark 7:24-30*). Like natural bread, believers need manna daily to receive nutrition and wellness from heaven. Though belivers receive deliverance and healing instantly, there are some matters that require ongoing maintenance and other methods of healing to bring deliverance. Believers need to embrace all that comes with their lifestyle journey of salvation with God. Believers need to seek these methods consistently to be healthy in their journey with the Lord.

- Have consistent supports and wise counselors, who journey in ministry with the minister; utilize these relationships as consistent pillars as this makes leaning on them in trying times easier.

- Schedule and commit to weekly, monthly, and yearly days of respite and sabbatical.
- Learn to identify burnout and weariness, and take respite as needed, to refresh, refocus, and renew in relationship with God, one's destiny, and calling.
- Have close supports who can help the minister identify they they need to take time to rest; trust their voices and take time to emotionally and physically recoup and heal as necessary.
- Avoid becoming the fixer to people as this positions the minister as God is people's lives, and causes ministry endeavors to be guided by unrealistic religious demands and false obligations.
- Get delivered from the spirit and mindsets of perfectionism. God requires us to live a life of excellency, while he perfects all that concerns us (*Psalms 138:8*). Perfectionism will have the minister fearing sharing struggles with those that can provide support, counsel, and deliverance; or pridefully rejecting or refusing to acquire assistance and/or deliverance when needed. Such a posture opens the door to make abrupt decisions to commit suicide.
- Build a sufficient team that can help with ministry duties and practices. Resist micromanaging the team. Build a team that can be trusted to carry the vision sufficiently.
- Be God led in the ministry vision, rather than guided by platform, fame, need for validation, religious doctrine, and people pleasing.
- Build and live through God identity and God confidence.

- Resist comparing self and ministry to others; minister as unto the Lord and not to keep up with the endeavors of other people.
- Free one's life from secret sin that cause condemnation and secretly being tormented by struggles and transgressions.
- Learn about warfare in order to identify psychological warfare, witchcraft attacks, and curses that can ensue suicidal ideation.
- Identify destiny killing spirits and how they operate against one's calling, and seasons of frustration, pruning, transition, success, and elevation. Destiny killing spirits tend to track a person throughout their life creating situations to thwart their destiny. These spirits can be the spirit of death and/or suicide or can open the door to them. Share this information with intercessors and confidants who can consistently pray to help thwart these attacks.

References:

≈ Olivetree.com
≈ Strongs Exhaustive Bible Concordance Online Bible Study Tools
≈ Suidical Signs & Symptoms from Medicalnewstoday.com

Be a Healthy You!

Kingdom Shifters Books & Apparel
Available at <u>Kingdomshifters.com</u>
<u>BOOKS FOR EVERYONE</u>

Healing The Wounded Leader

Kingdom Shifters Decree That Thang

There Is An App For That

Kingdom Watchman Builder On The Wall

Embodiment Of A Kingdom Watchman

Dismantling Homosexuality Handbook

Release The Vision

Kingdom Heirs Decree That Thang

Birthing Books That Shift Generations

Let There Be Sight

Atmosphere Changers (Weaponry)

Apostolic Governing

Apostolic Mantle

Dance From Heaven To Earth

Annihilating Church Hurt

Discerning The Voice of God

Feasting In His Presence

Prayers That Shift Atmospheres

<u>BOOKS FOR DANCERS</u>
Dancers! Dancers! Dancers! Decree That Thang

Spirits That Attack Dance Ministers & Ministries

Dance & Fivefold Ministry

Dance From Heaven To Earth

<u>CD'S</u>
Decree That Thang CD

Kingdom Heirs Decree That Thang CD

Teaching & Worship CD's